Dtp
and
graphic design

Iacob Adrian

Louvre
Color Plates
STUDY
vol. 1

Iacob Adrian

ISBN-13 : 978-1479130511
ISBN-10 : 1479130516

LIST OF PICTURES

ARTIST	TITLE
LEONARDO DA VINCI	PORTRAIT OF MONA LISA (LA JOCONDE)
SIMONE MARTINI	CHRIST BEARING HIS CROSS
FRA FILIPPO LIPPI	MADONNA AND CHILD, WITH ANGELS, AND TWO ABBOTS
DOMENICO GHIRLANDAIO	PORTRAIT OF AN OLD MAN AND HIS GRANDSON (THE BOTTLE-NOSED MAN)
BOTTICELLI	GIOVANNA DEGLI ALBIZZI AND THE THREE GRACES
PERUGINO	ST. SEBASTIAN
RAPHAEL	LA BELLE JARDINIERE
RAPHAEL	PORTRAIT OF BALDASSARE CASTIGLIONE
ANTONELLO DA MESSINA	PORTRAIT OF A CONDOTTIERE
GIORGIONE	PASTORAL SYMPHONY
PALMA VECCHIO	THE ADORATION OF THE SHEPHERDS, WITH A FEMALE DONOR
TITIAN	THE MAN WITH A GLOVE
TITIAN	THE ENTOMBMENT (La Mise au Tombeau)
ANDREA MANTEGNA	PARNASSUS
CORREGGIO	THE MYSTIC MARRIAGE OF ST. CATHERINE
JAN VAN EYCK	THE VIRGIN AND CHILD AND THE CHANCELLOR BOLIN
HANS MEMLINC	PORTRAIT OF AN OLD LADY
GEEAED DAVID	THE MARRIAGE AT CANA
QUENTIN MATSYS	THE BANKER AND HIS WIFE
JAN MABUSE	PORTRAIT OF JEAN CARONDELET
RUBENS	HENRI IV. LEAVES FOR THE WAR WITH GERMANY
RUBENS	PORTRAIT OF HELENS FOURMENT AND TWO OF HER CHILDREN.
VAN DYCK	PORTRAIT OF KING CHARLES I. OF ENGLAND
HANS HOLBEIN THE YOUNGER	PORTRAIT OF ERASMUS
VELAZQUEZ	PORTRAIT OF THE INFANTA MARGARITA
MURILLO	THE IMMACULATE CONCEPTION

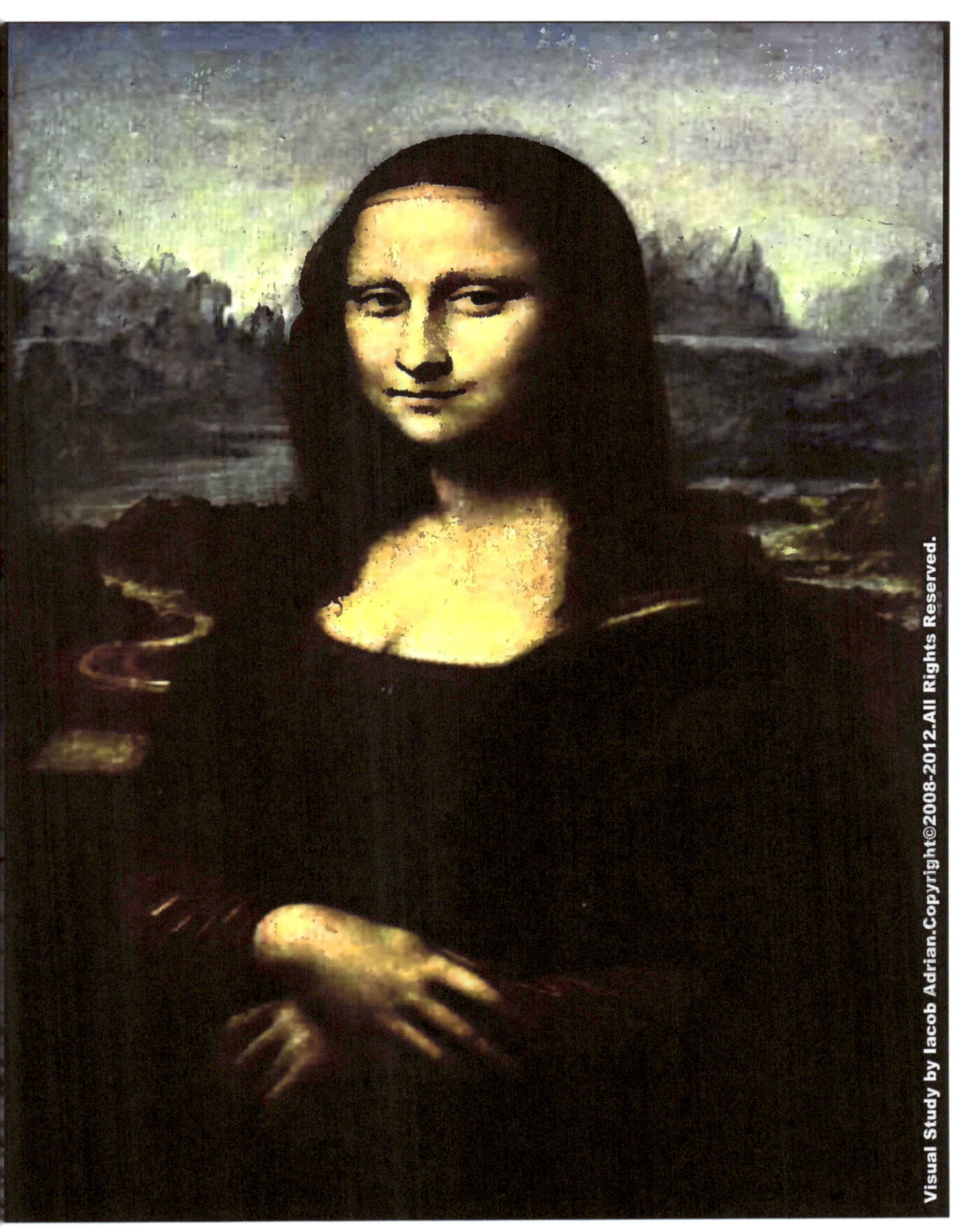

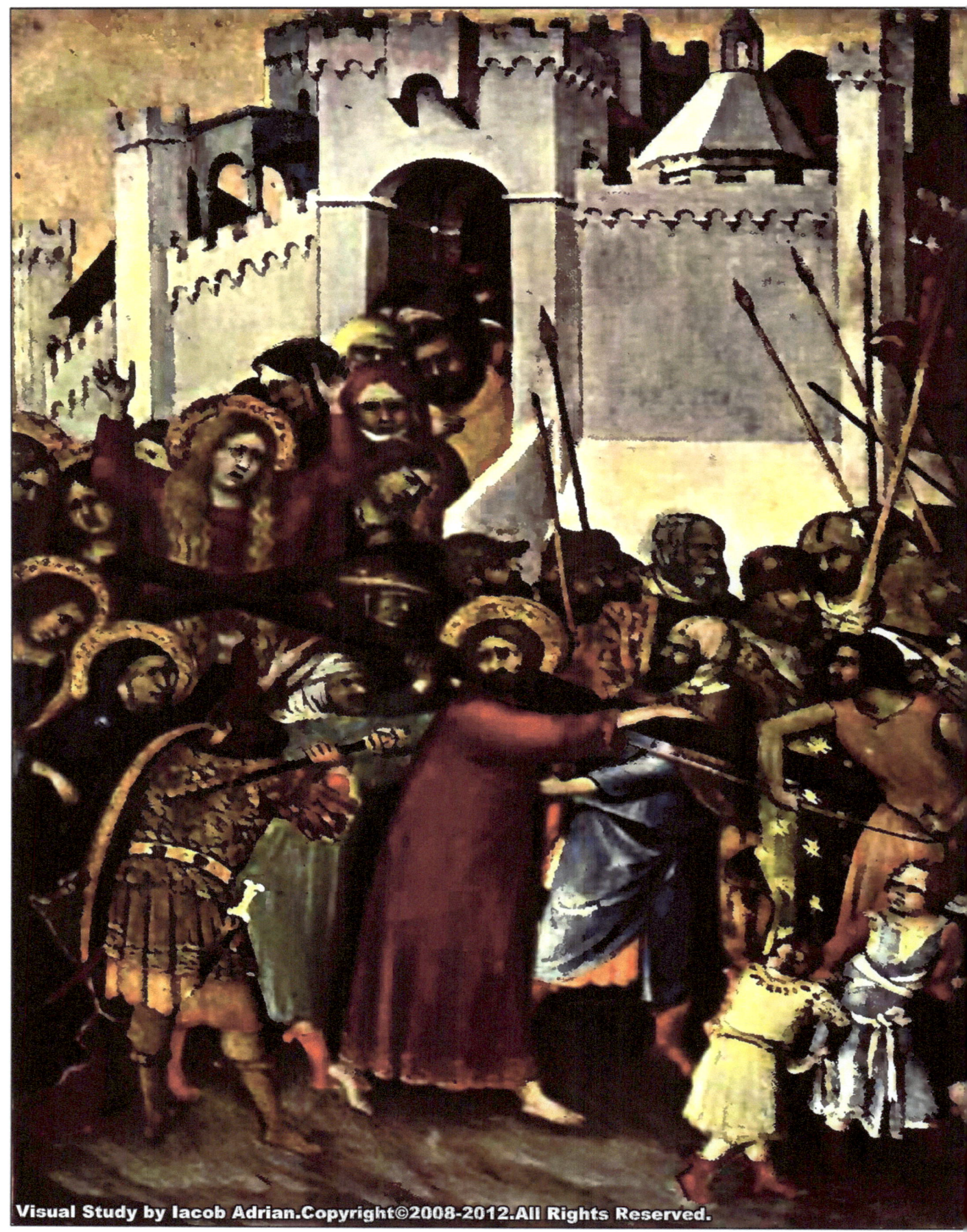

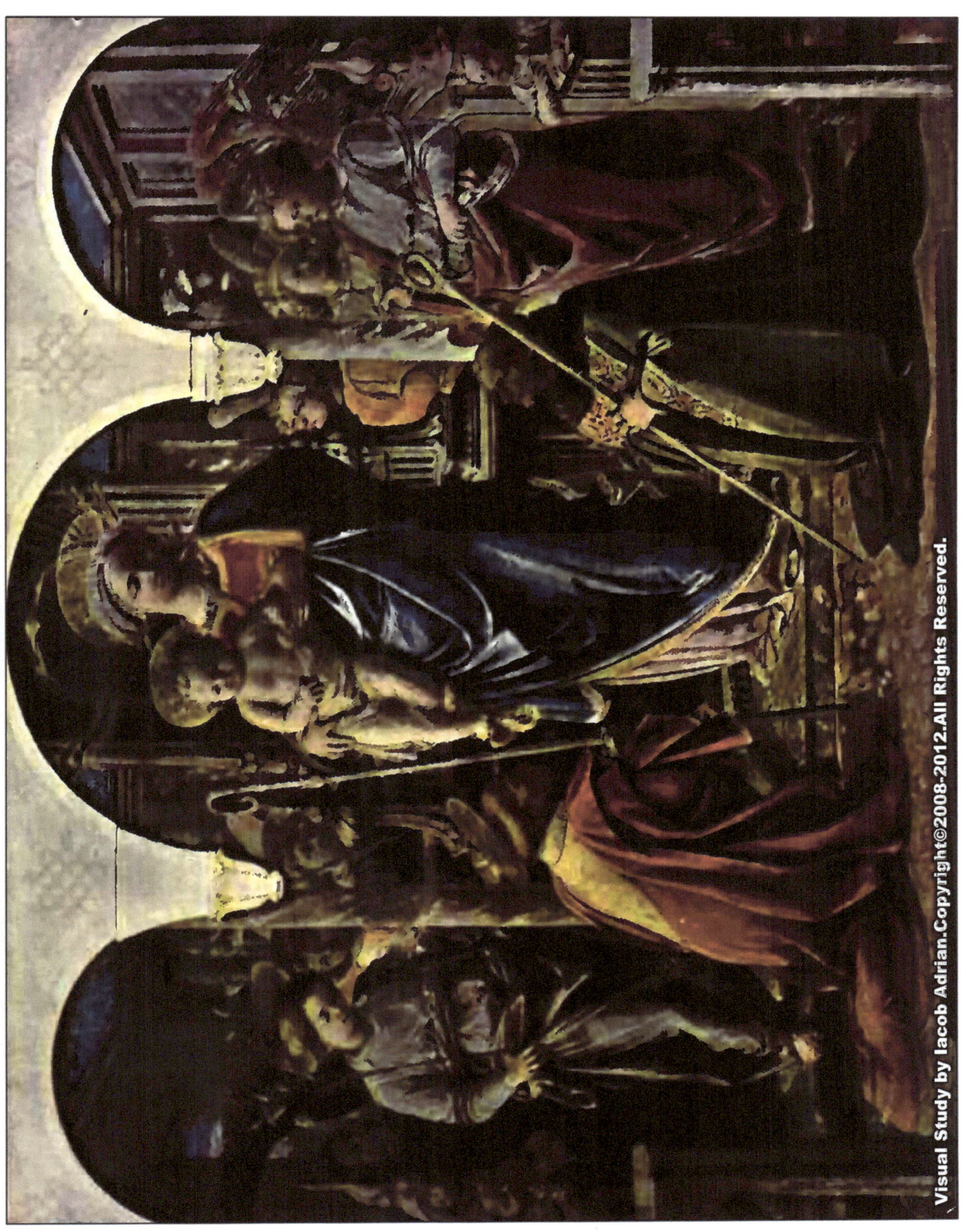

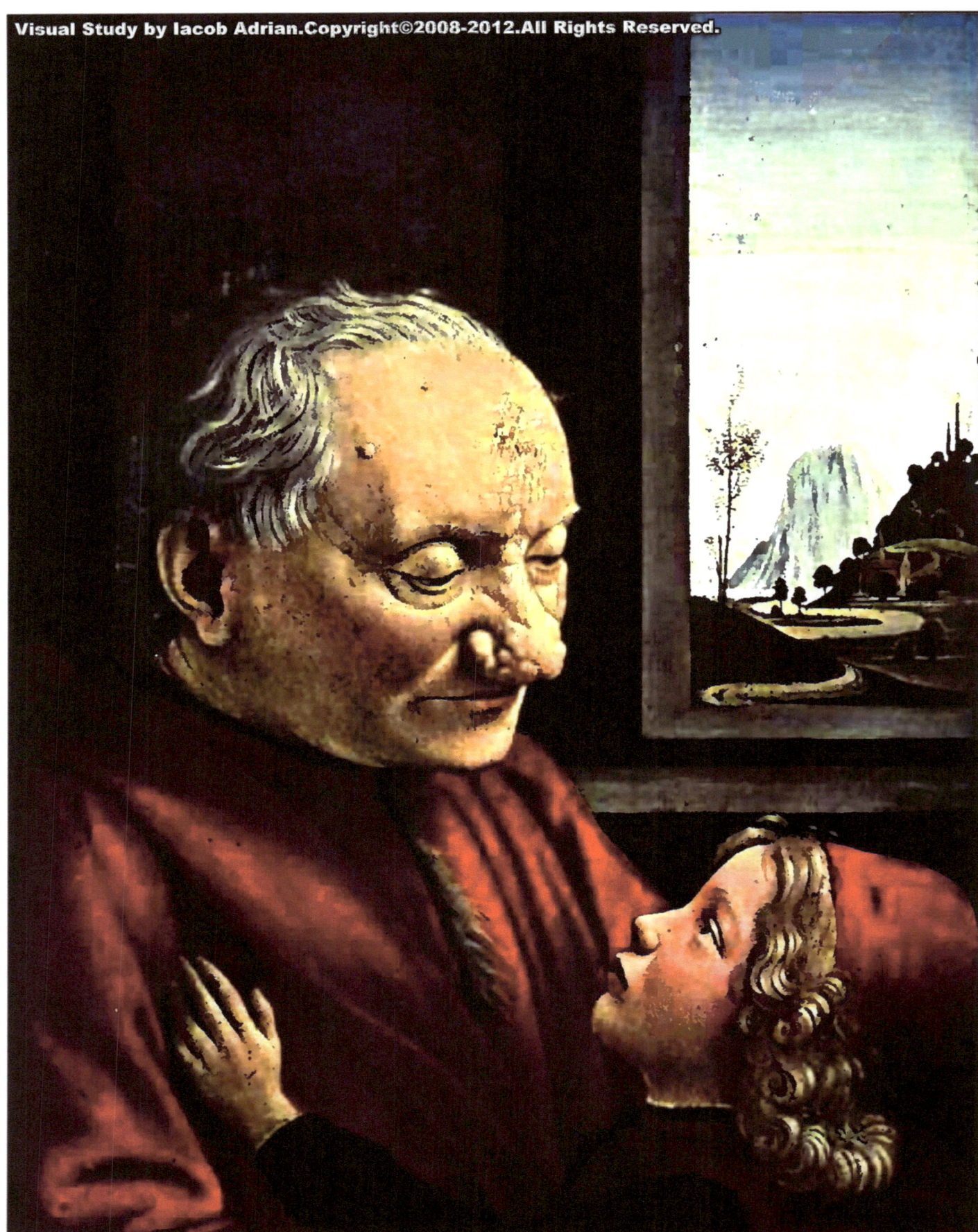

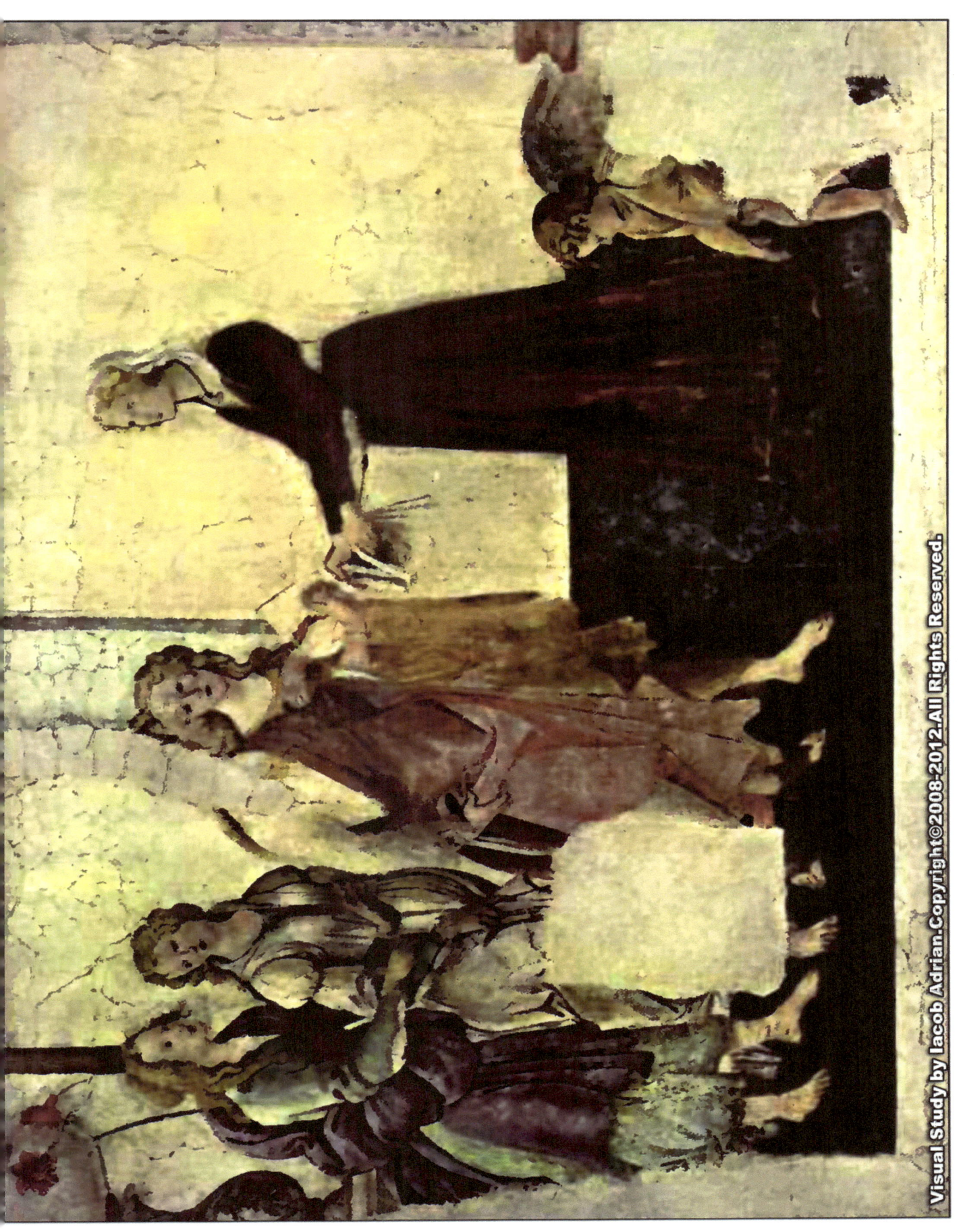

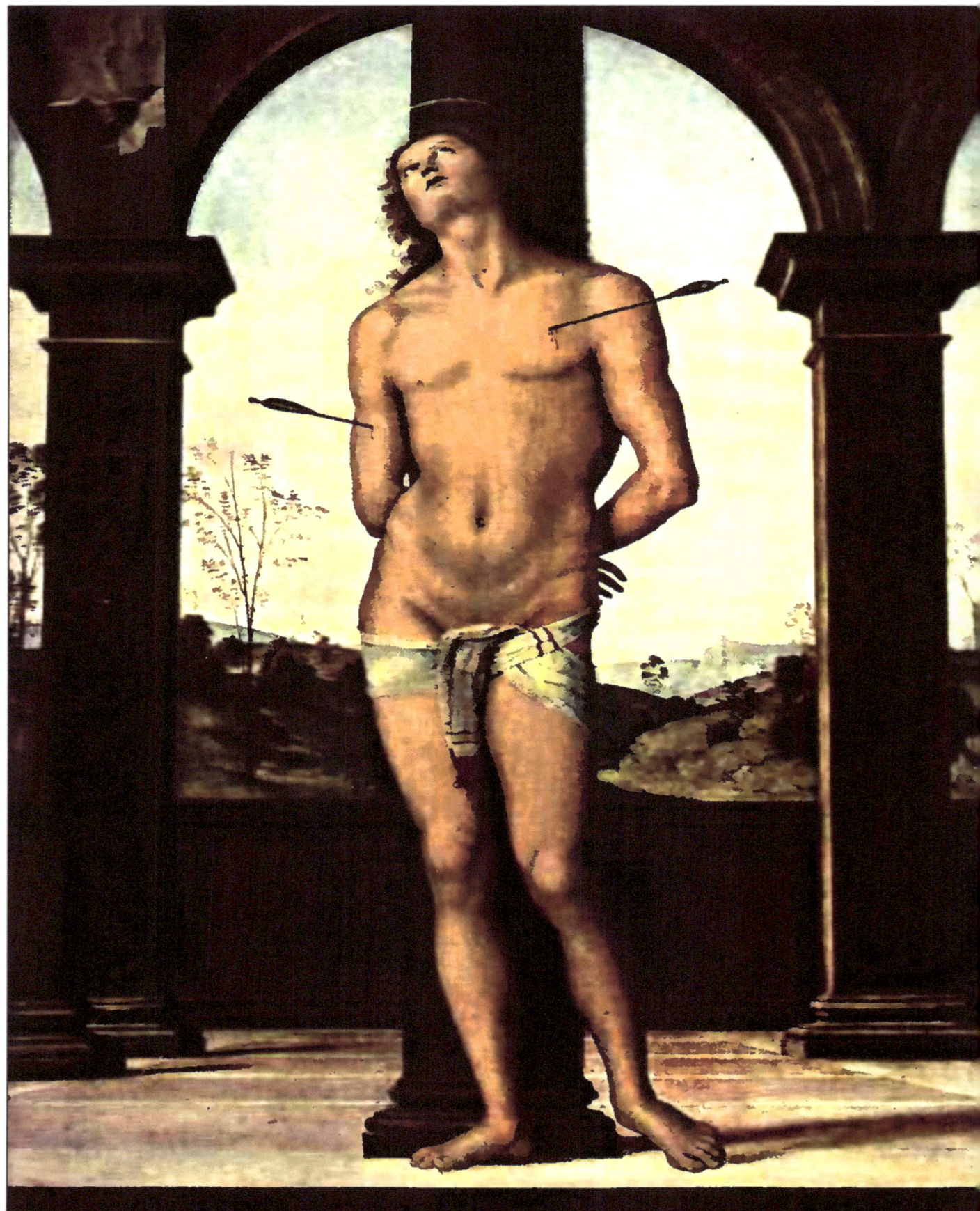

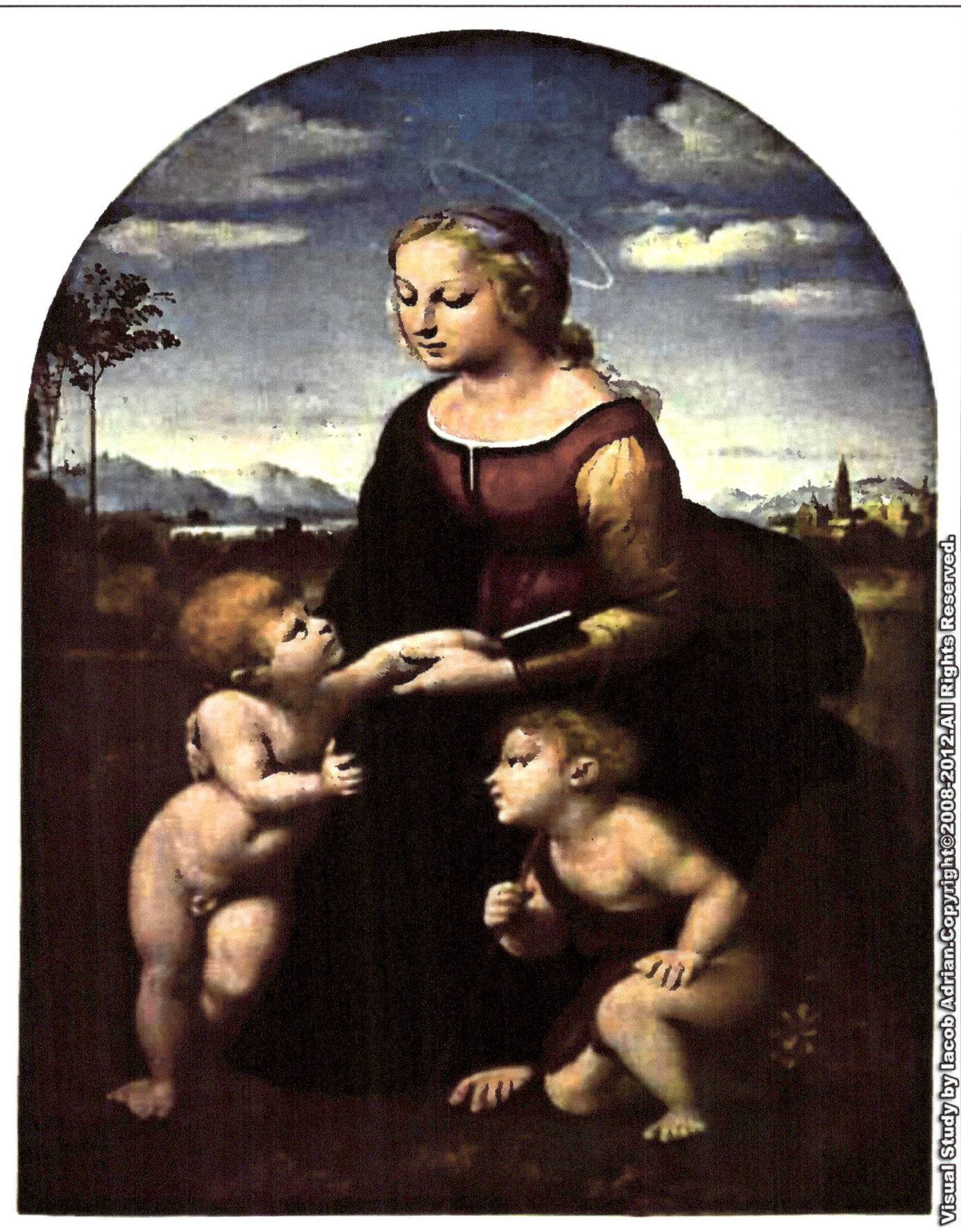

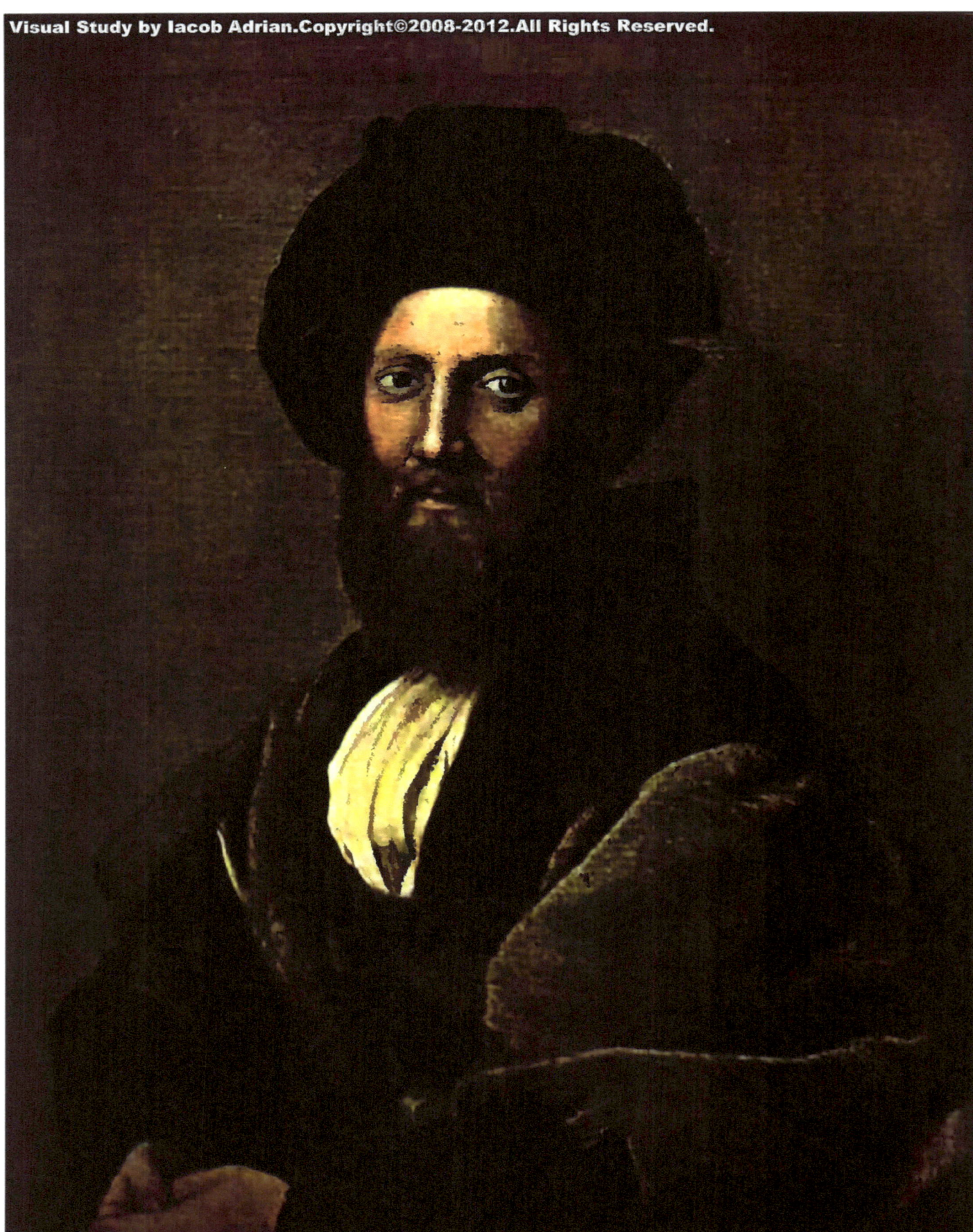

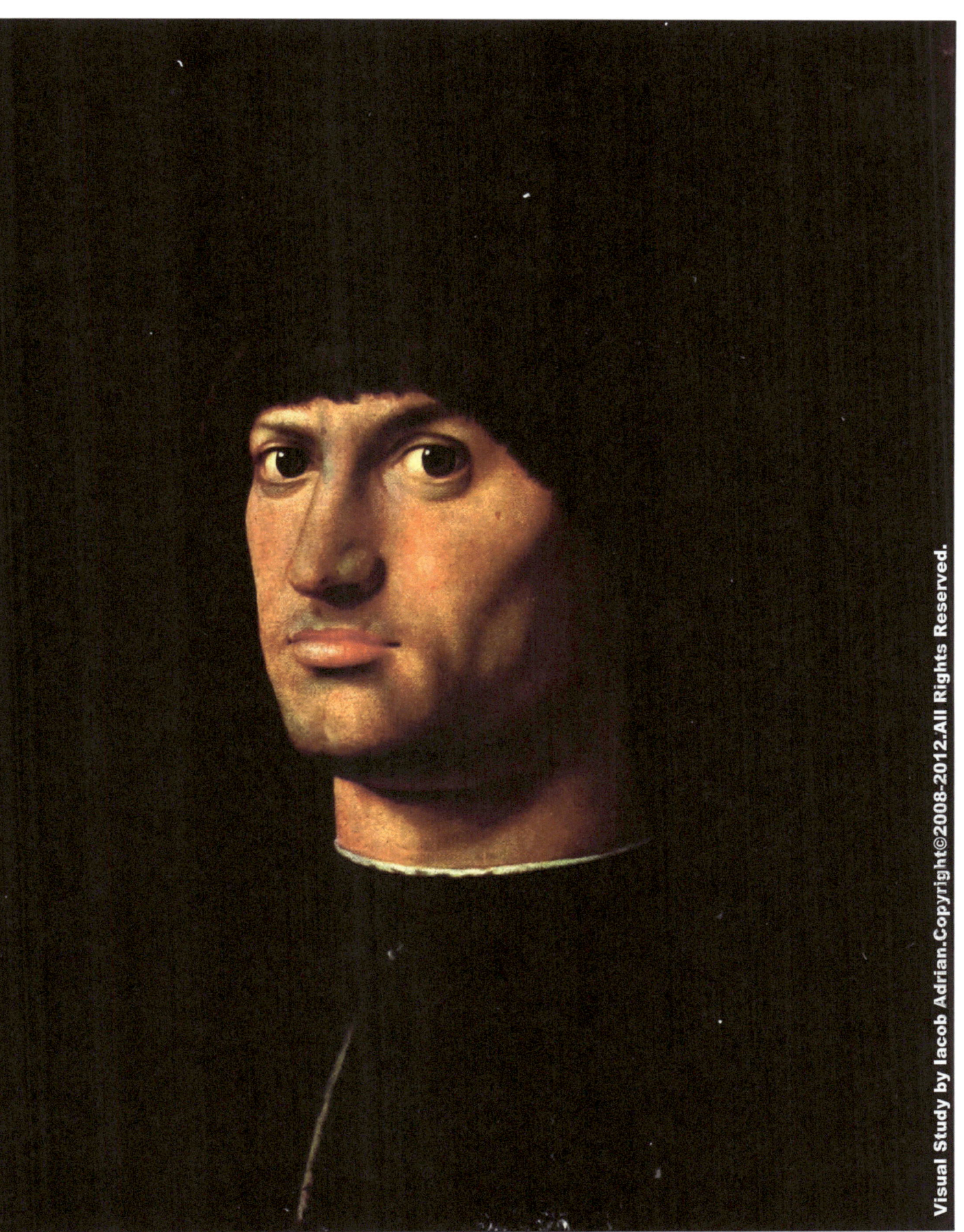

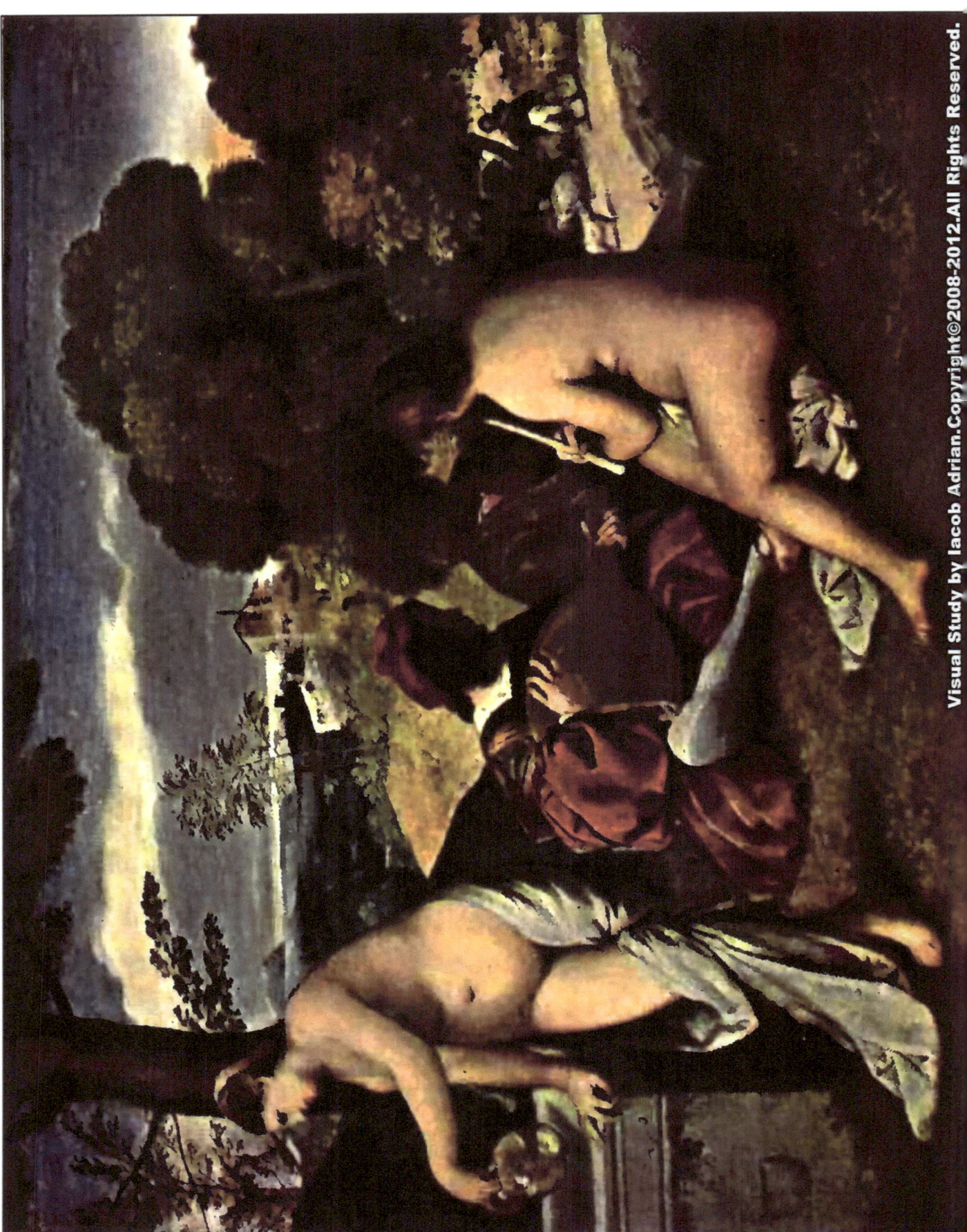

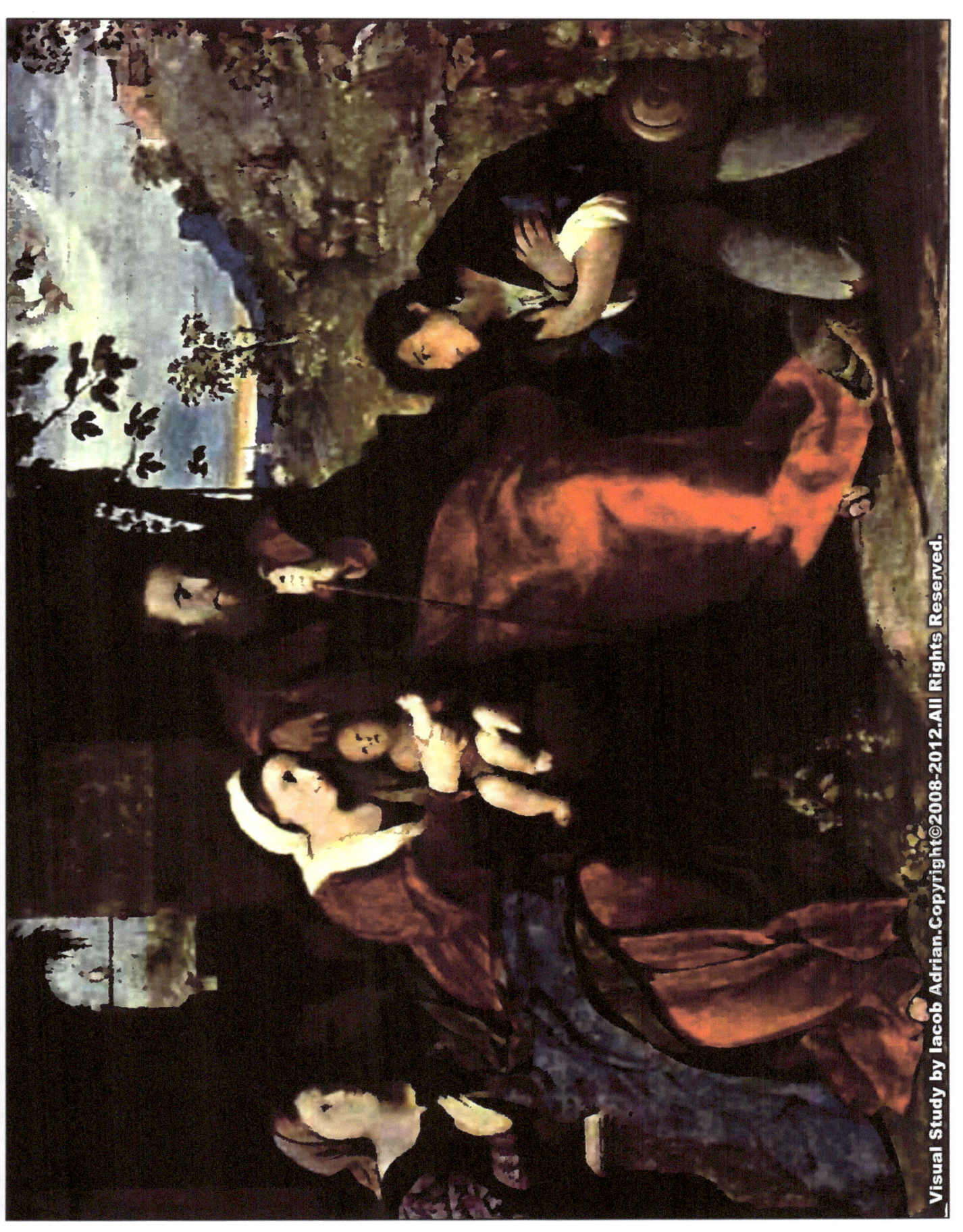

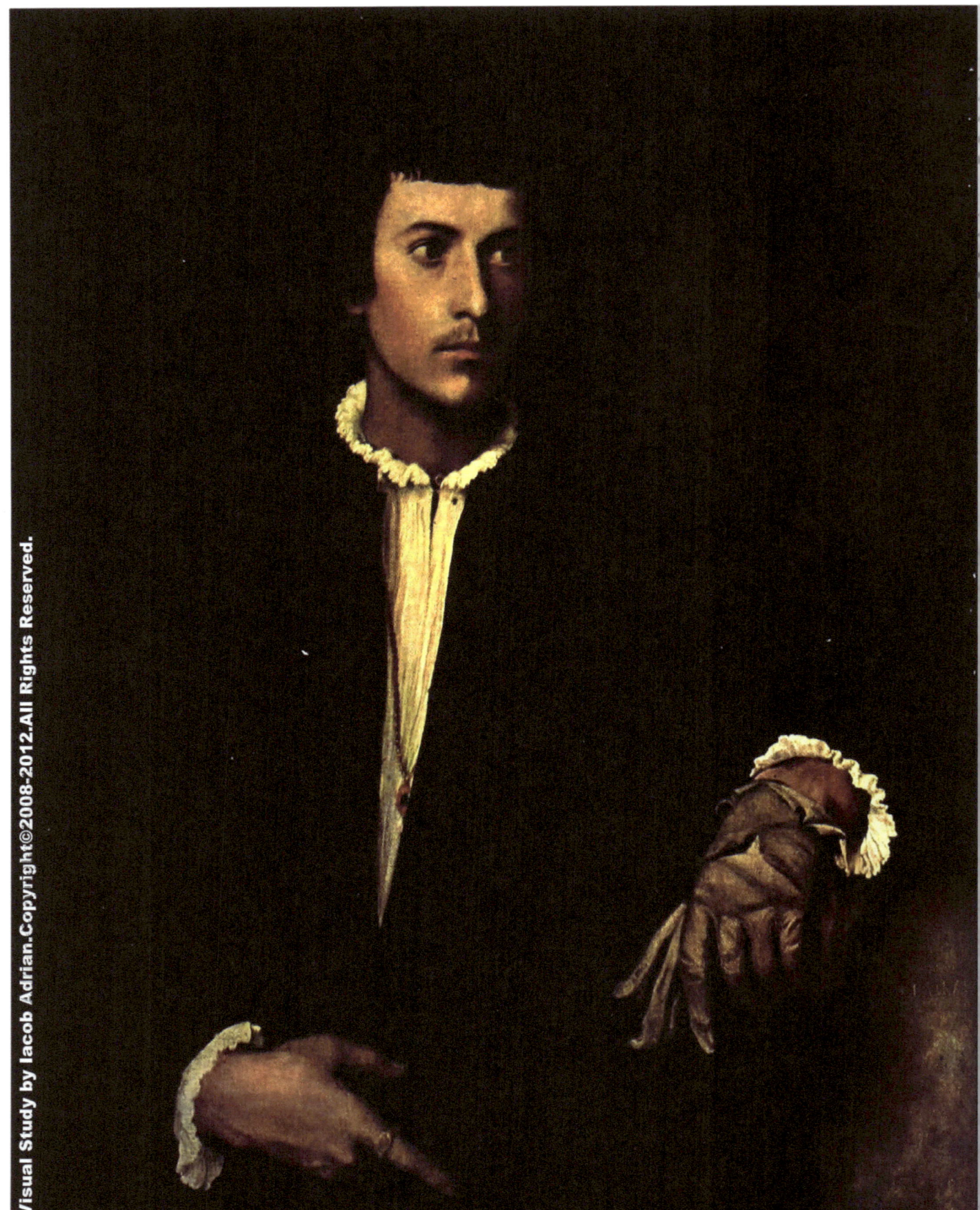

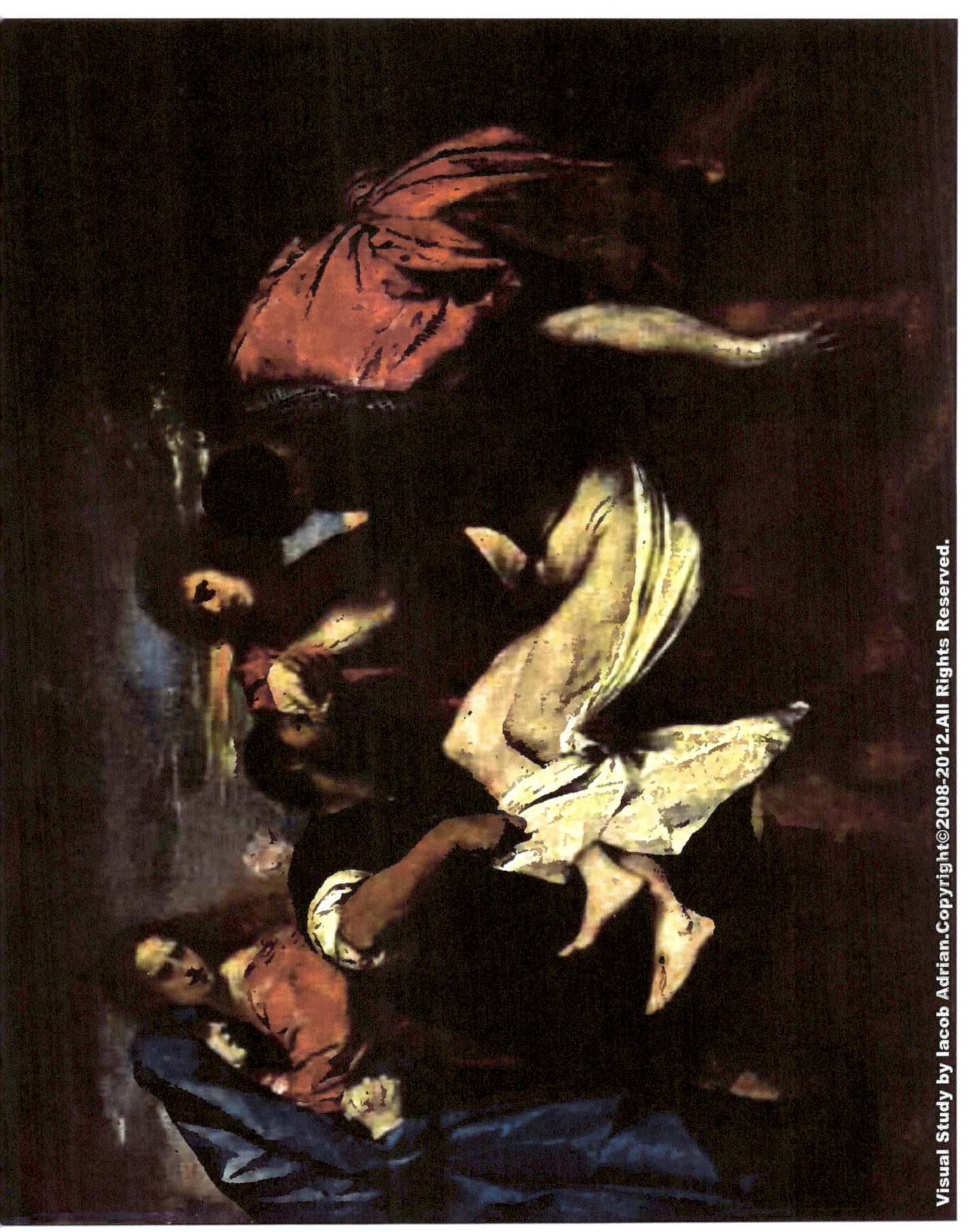

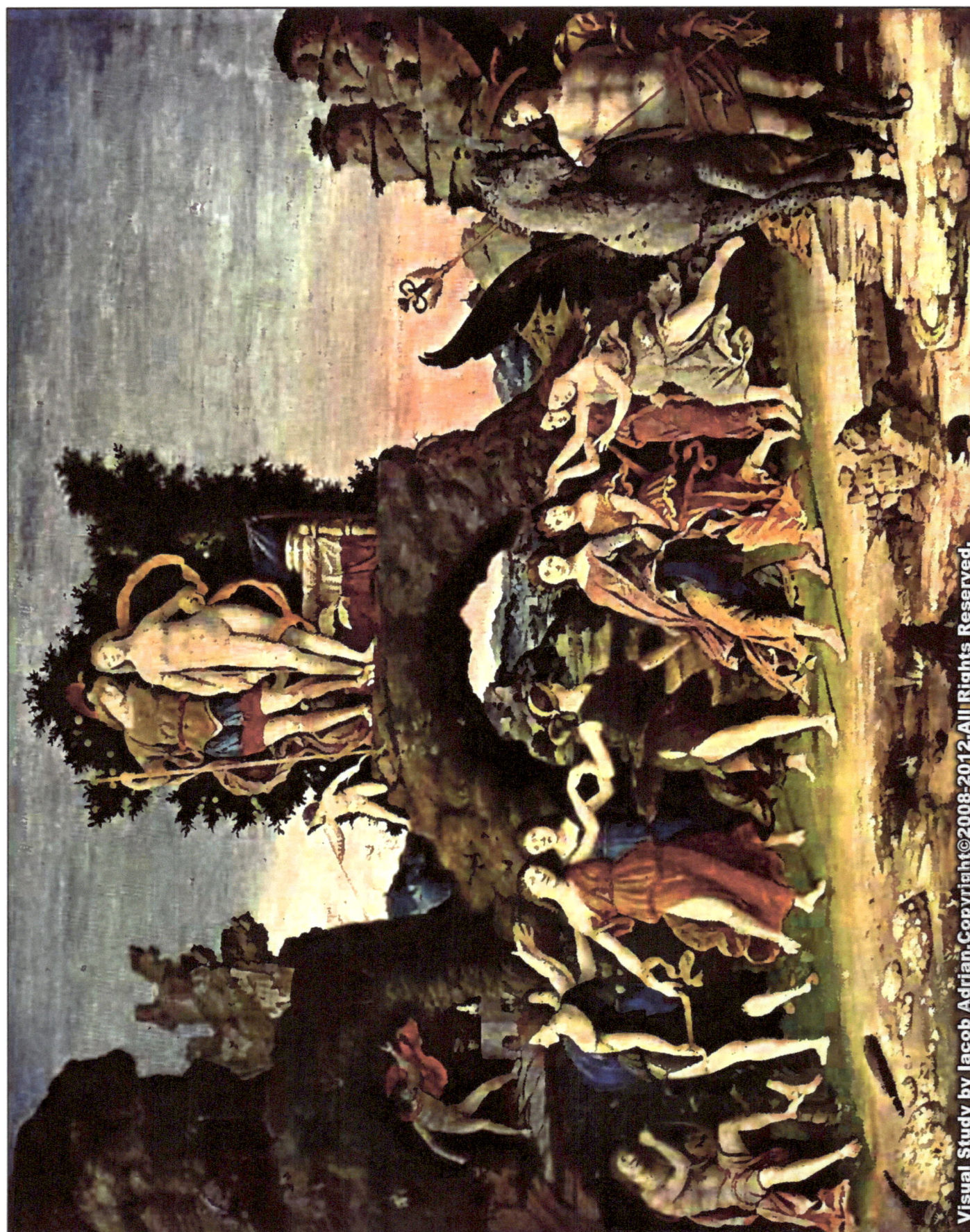

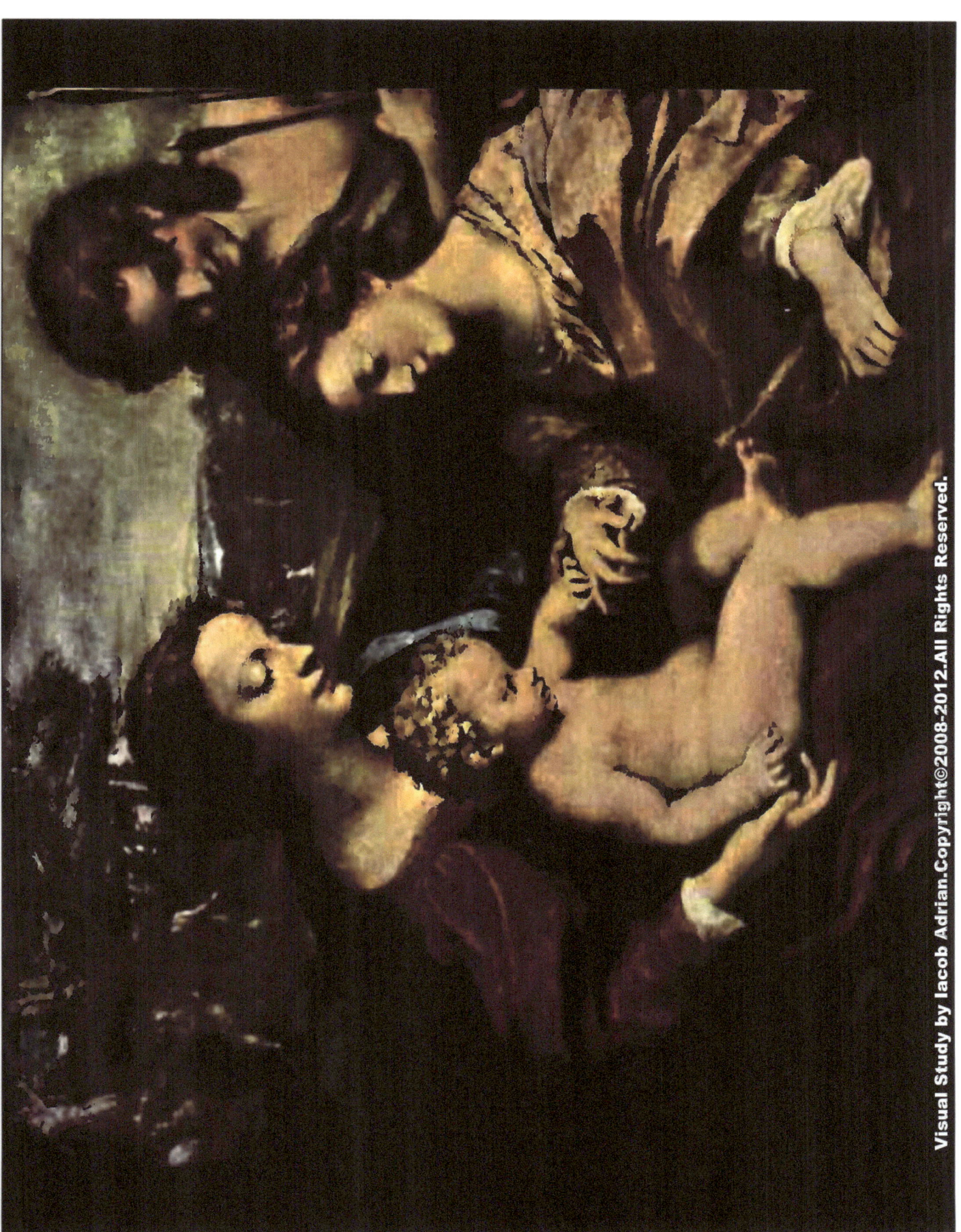

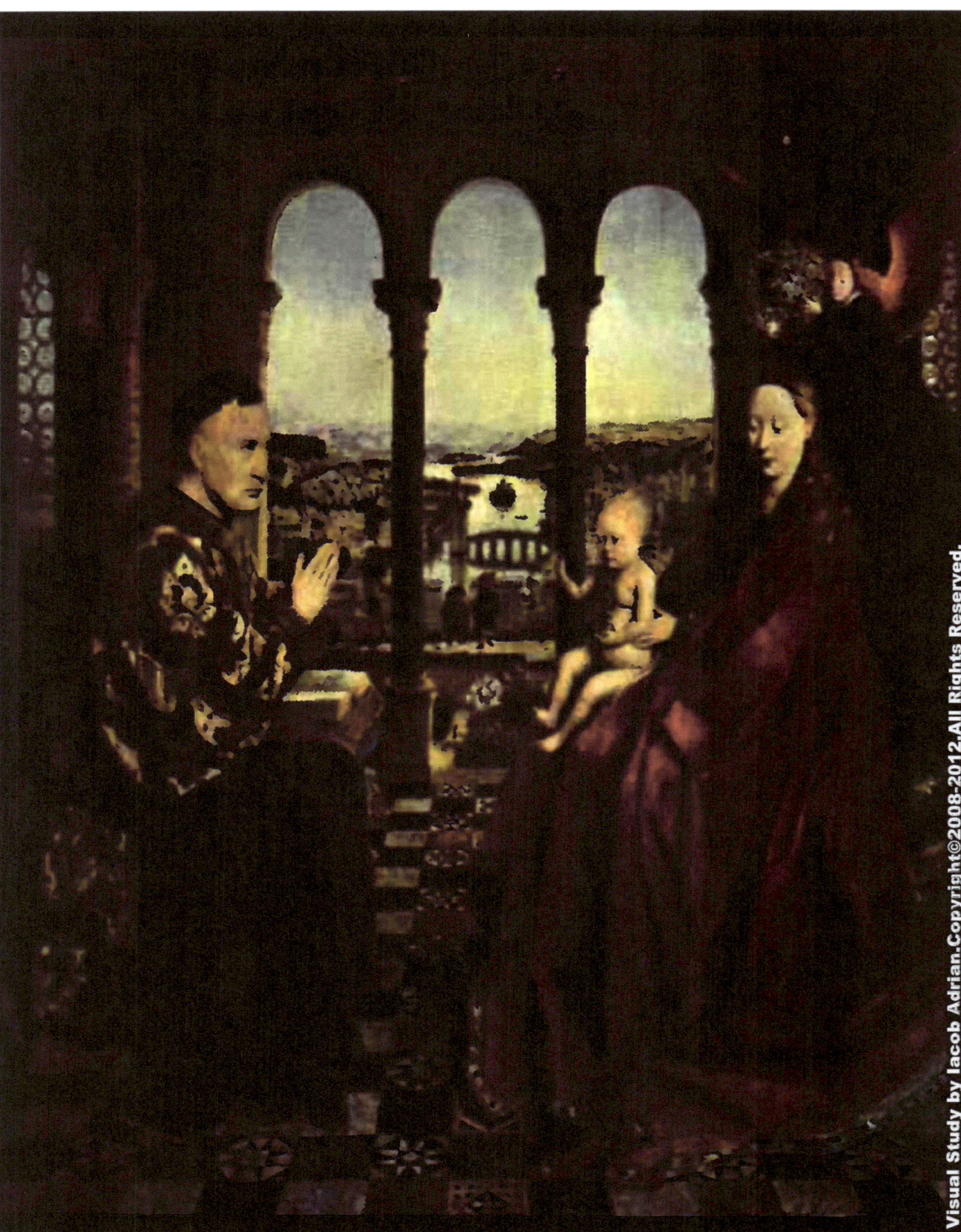

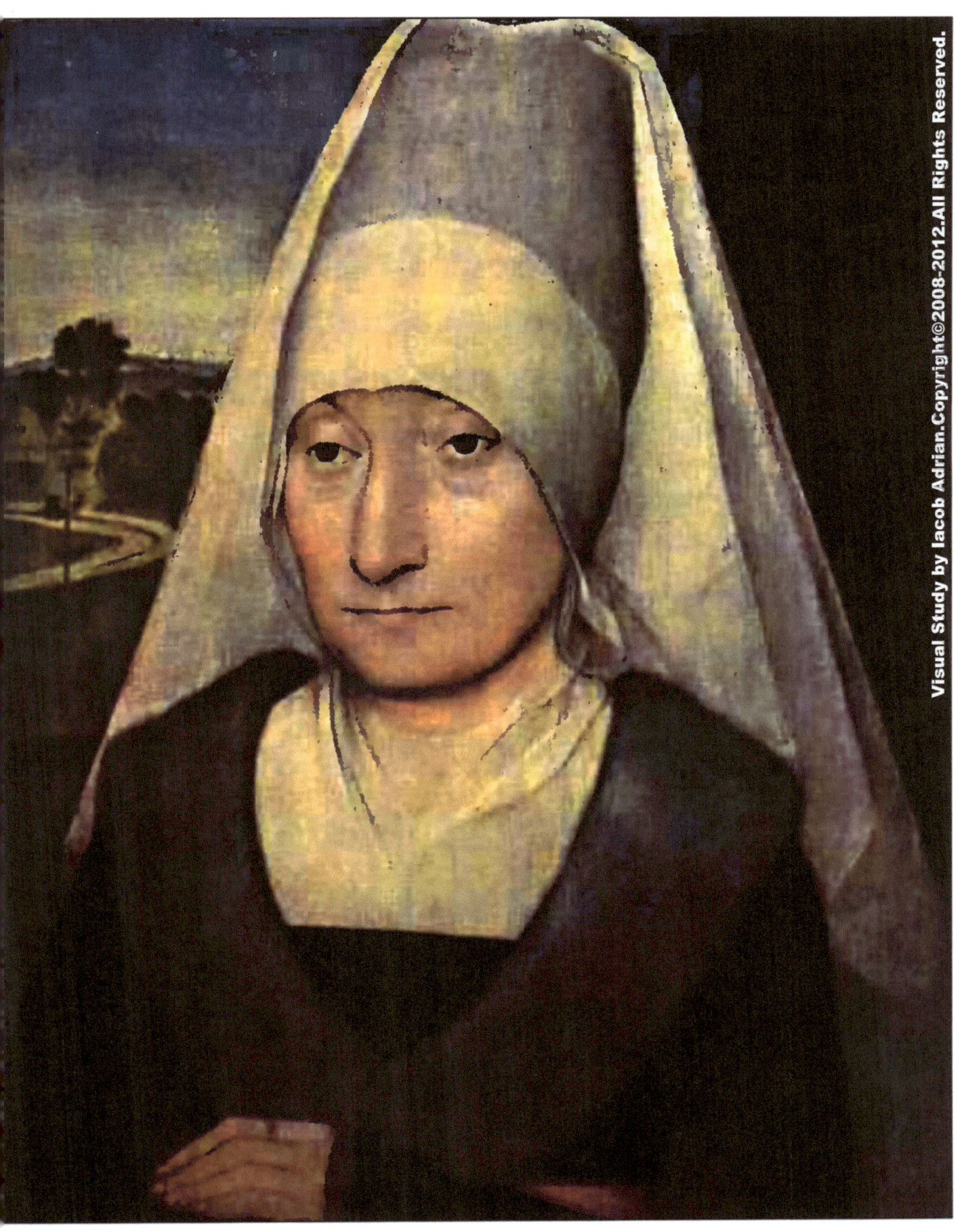

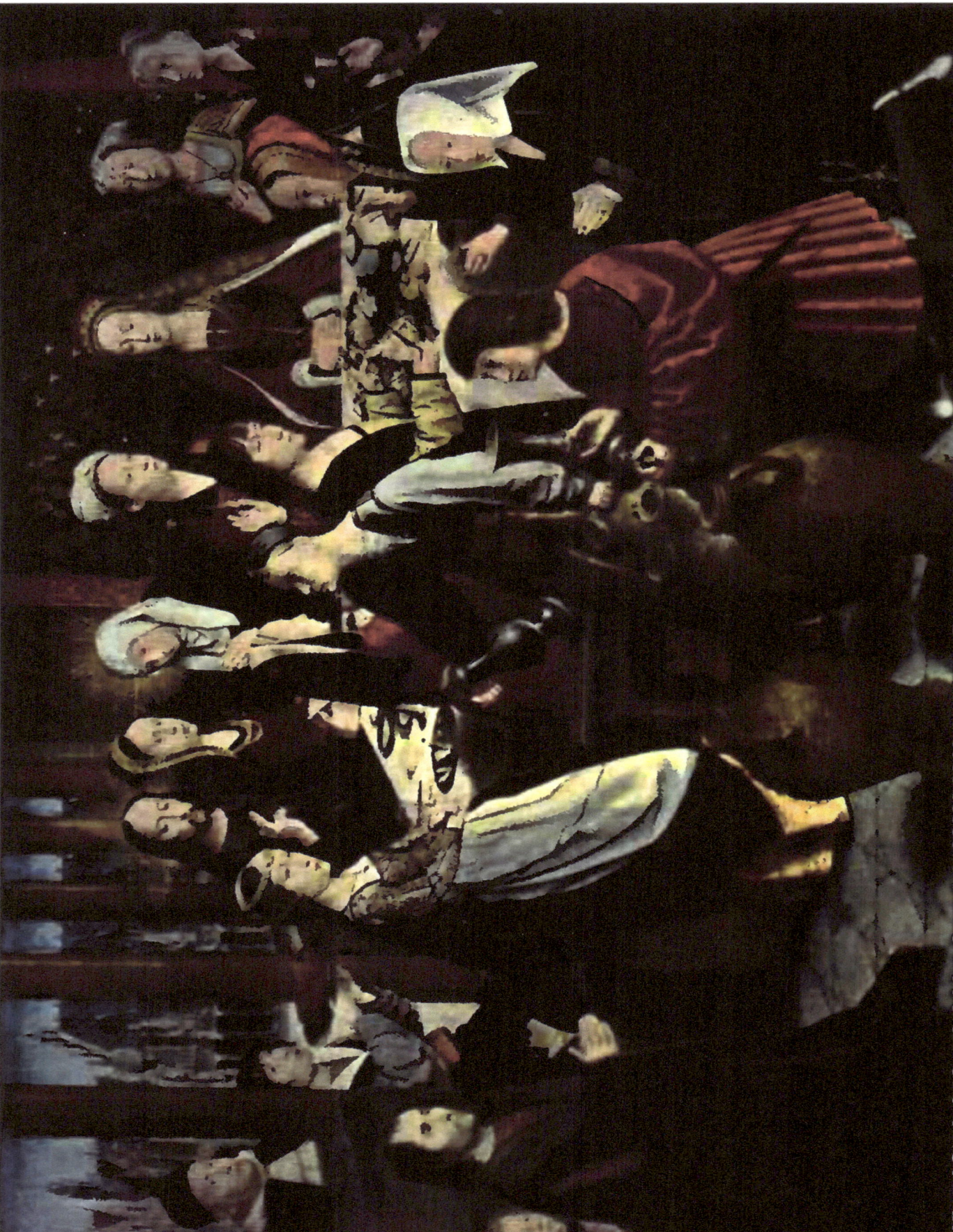

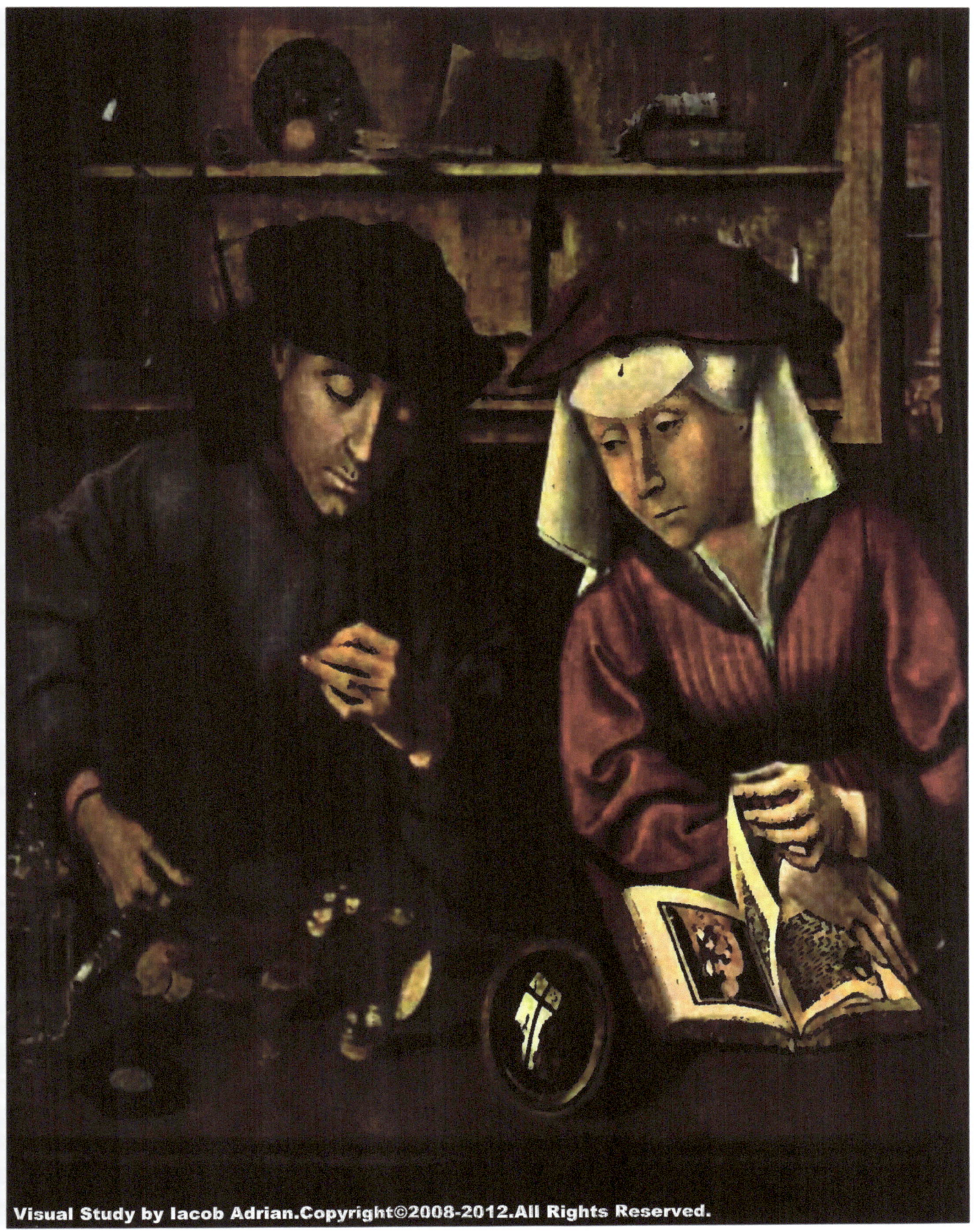

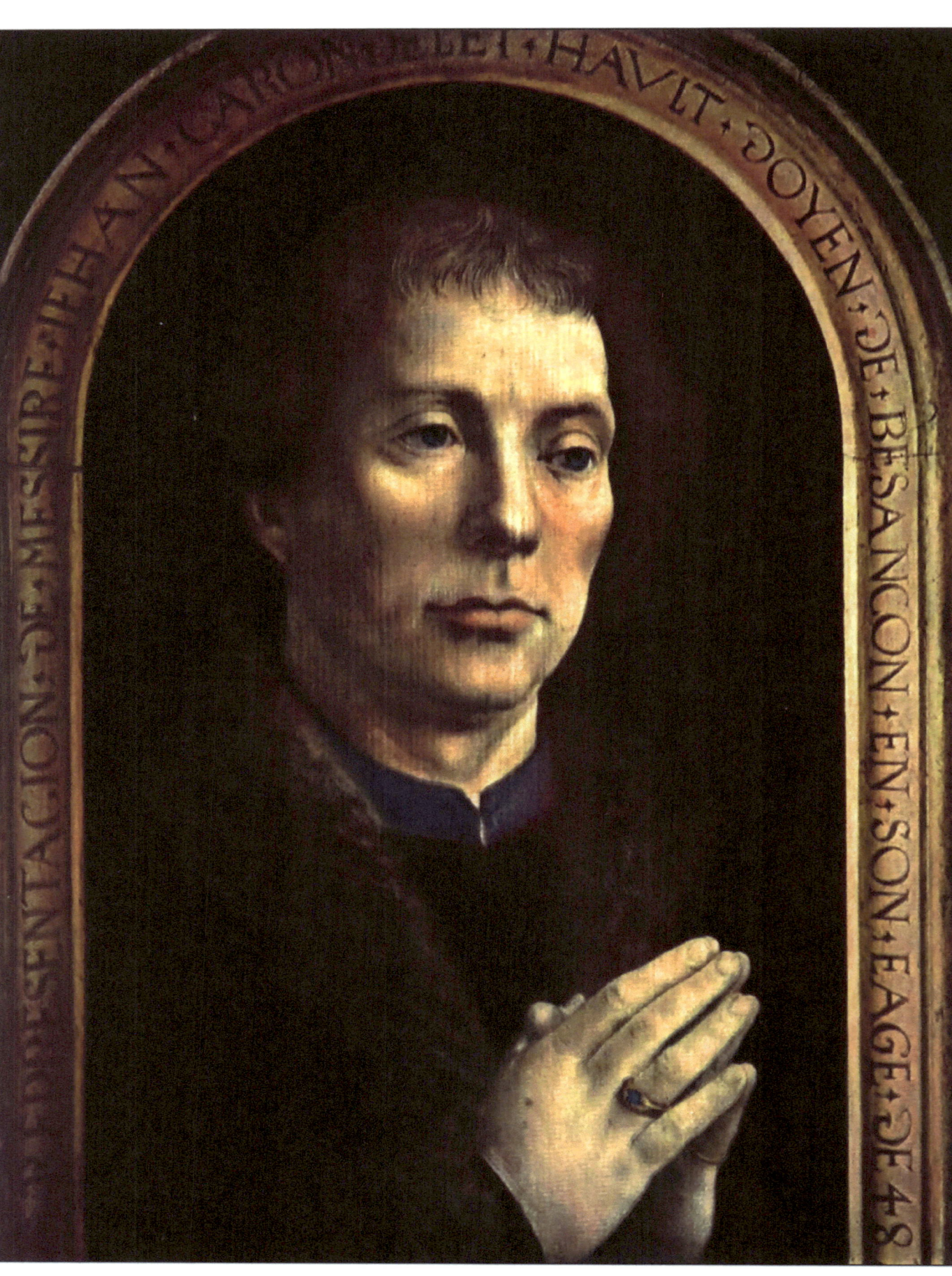

+PRESENTACION+DE+MESSIRE+FHAN+CARONDELET+HAVLT+DOYEN+DE+BESANCON+EN+SON+EAGE+DE+48

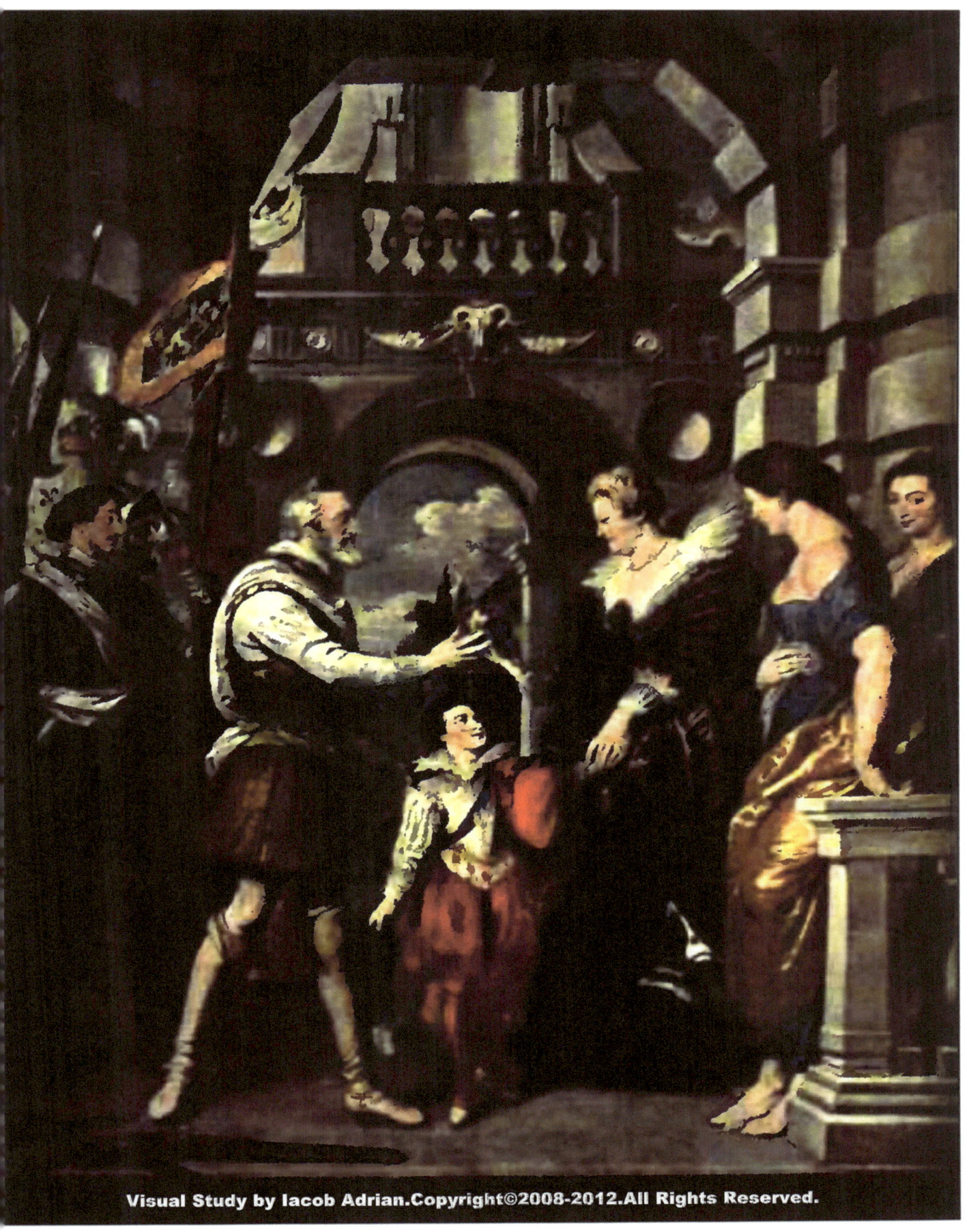

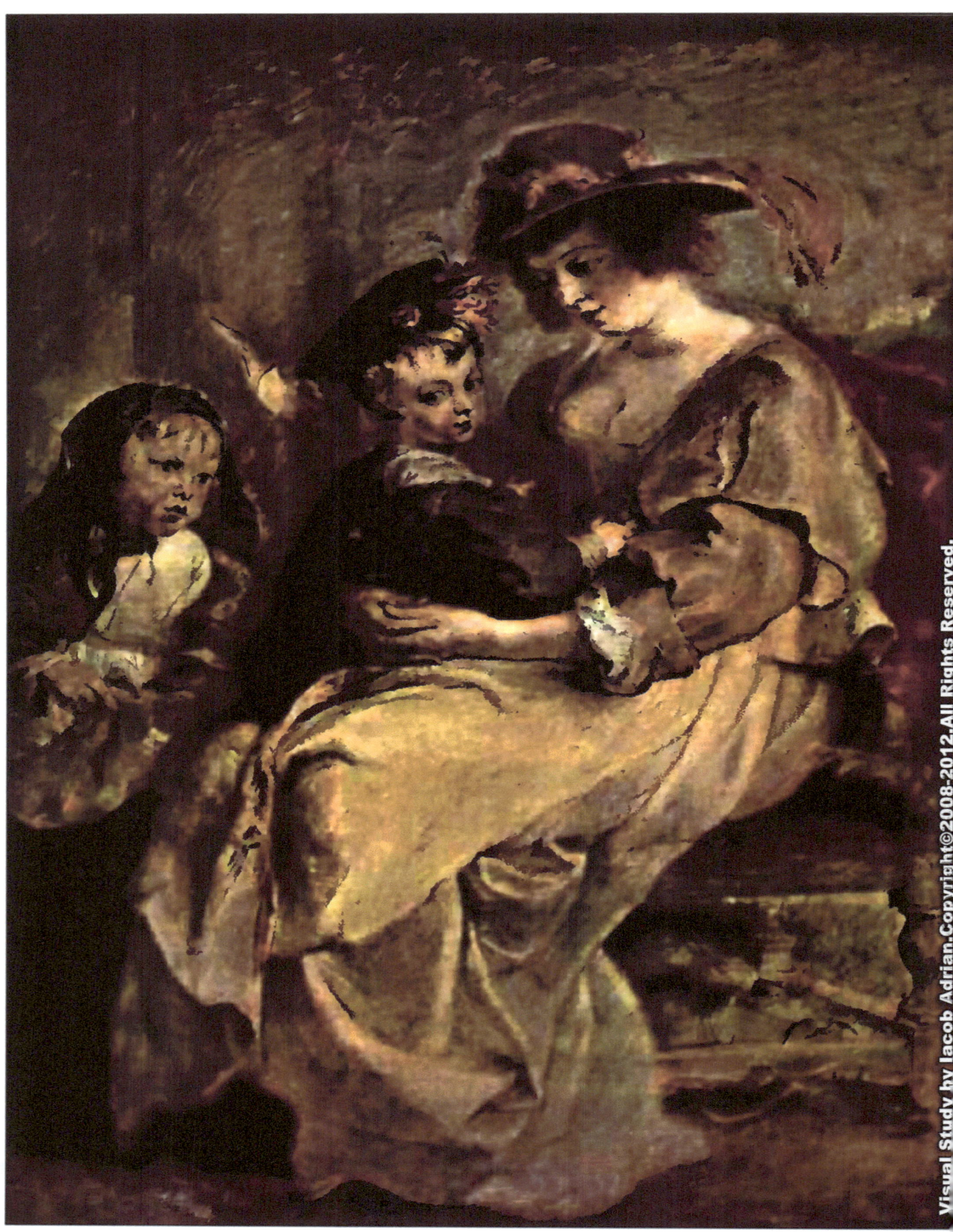

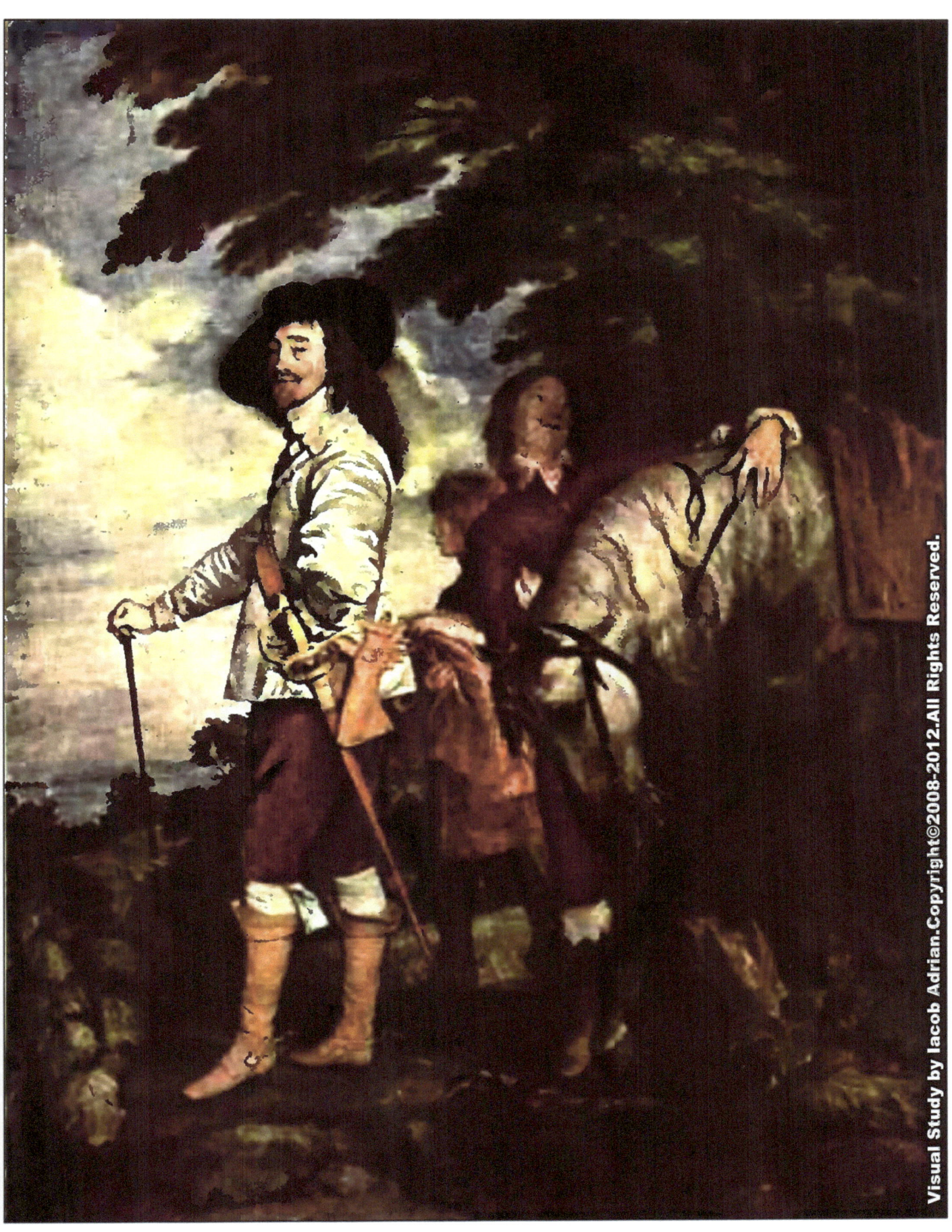

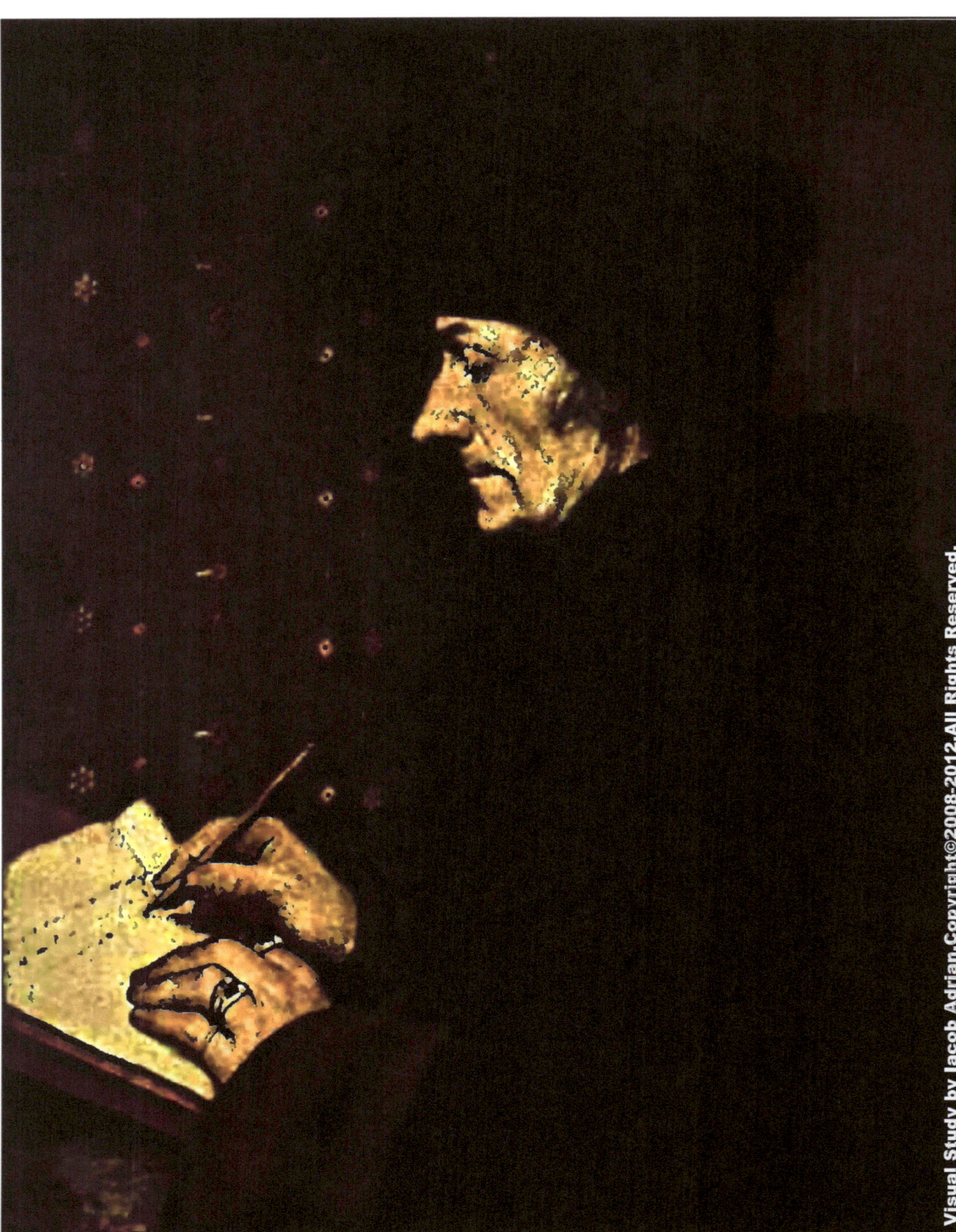

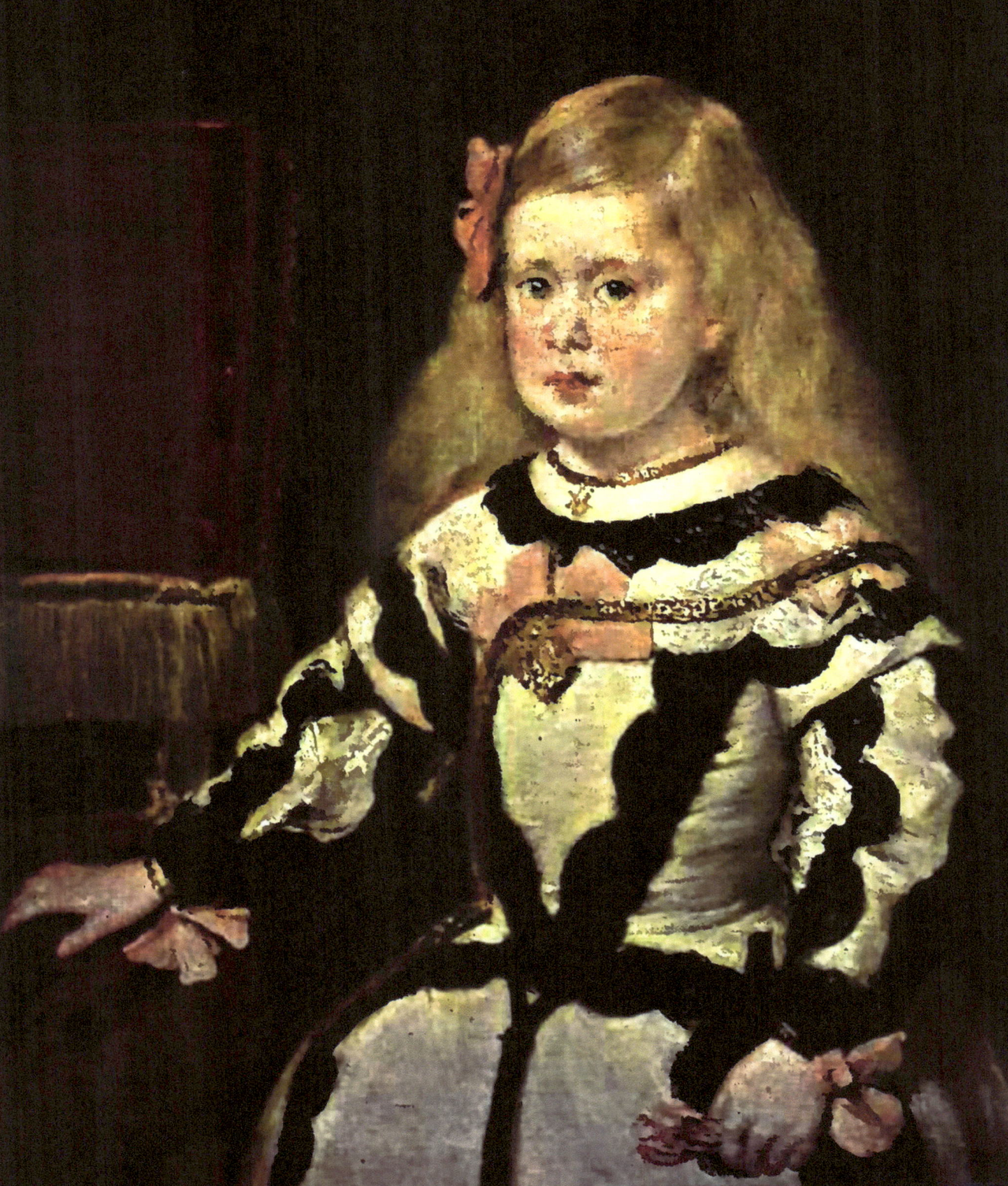

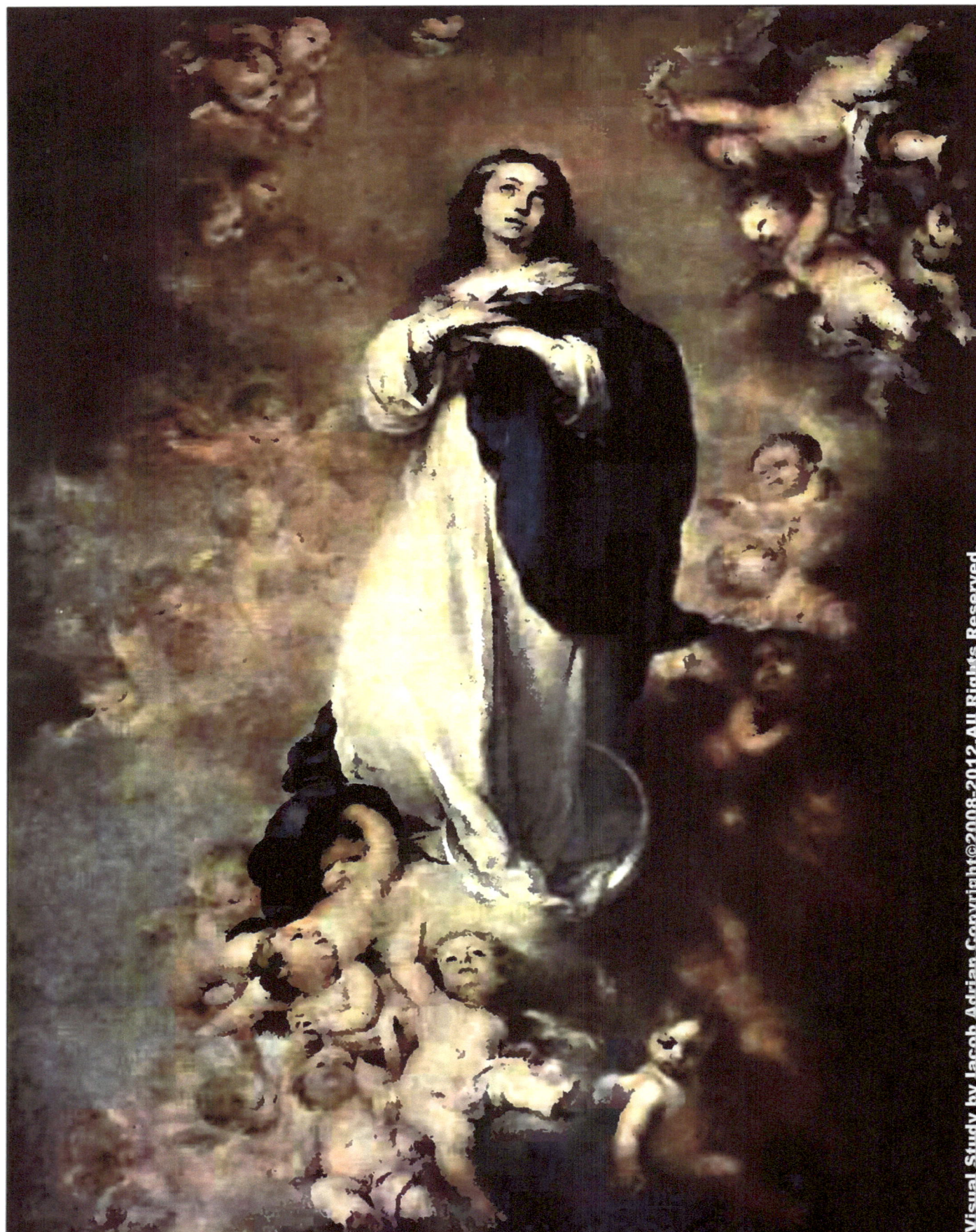

Bibliographic sources :

The Louvre; fifty plates in colour; (1911)

Author: Konody, Paul G. (Paul George), 1872-1933; Brockwell, M. W
Publisher: New York, Dodge

The Louvre: fifty plates in colour. By Paul G. Konody and Maurice W. Brockwell.
Editor: T. Leman Hare (1910)

Author: Konody, Paul G. (Paul George), 1872-1933; Brockwell, Maurice Walter, 1869-1958;
Hare, Thomas Leman, 1872-
Publisher: London T.C. & E.C. Jack